Insects
and
Spiders

Spiders

Shane F McEvey
for the Australian Museum

This edition first published in 2002 in the United States of America by Chelsea House Publishers, a subsidiary of Haights Cross Communications.

Chelsea House Publishers
1974 Sproul Road, Suite 400
Broomall, PA 19008-0914

The Chelsea House world wide web address is www.chelseahouse.com

Library of Congress Cataloging-in-Publication Data Applied for.

ISBN 0-7910-6599-5

First published in 2001 by
Macmillan Education Australia Pty Ltd
627 Chapel Street, South Yarra, Australia, 3141

Copyright © Australian Museum Trust 2001
Copyright in photographs © individual photographers as credited

Edited by Anna Fern
Text design by Nina Sanadze
Cover design by Nina Sanadze
Australian Museum Publishing Unit: Jennifer Saunders and Catherine Lowe
Australian Museum Series Editor: Deborah White

Printed in China

Acknowledgements

Our thanks to Mike Gray and Margaret Humphrey for helpful discussion and comments.

The author and the publisher are grateful to the following for permission to reproduce copyright material:

Cover: A mouse spider, photo by Robert Valentic/Nature Focus.

Andrew Davoll/Lochman Transparencies, p. 20 (right); Australian Museum/Nature Focus, pp. 26 (right), 27; D. Knowles/Lochman Transparencies. p. 25 (right); Dennis Sarson/Lochman Transparencies, pp. 9 (right), 12 (top), 15 (top right), 19 (middle and bottom), 21 (bottom), 23 (middle), 25 (left), 29 (bottom); Densey Clyne/Mantis Wildlife, pp. 24, 28 (right); Dominic Chaplin/Nature Focus, p. 30; Jim Frazier/Mantis Wildlife, p. 11 (top); Jiri Lochman/Lochman Transparencies, pp. 8 (top), 10 (bottom), 12 (bottom), 13 (top and middle), 17 (top), 22 (top and bottom), 26 (left), 28 (left); Michael Cermak/Nature Focus, pp. 7 (top), 11 (bottom), 14 (top); Mike Gray/Nature Focus, pp. 5 (right), 9 (left), 14 (bottom), 18 (top and bottom), 19 (top), 20 (left), 21 (middle), 23 (top and bottom); Pavel German/Nature Focus, pp. 8 (bottom), 15 (bottom), 18 (middle), 21 (top), 29 (top); Peter Marsack/Lochman Transparencies, p. 22 (middle); Phillip Griffin/Nature Focus, p. 13 (bottom); Robert Valentic/Nature Focus, pp. 5 (left), 6–7, 10 (top); Stephen Richards/Nature Focus, p. 16 (top); Steve Wilson, pp. 4, 16 (bottom), 17 (bottom); Wade Hughes/Lochman Transparencies, p. 15 (top left).

Contents

What are spiders?   4

Spider bodies   6

Where do spiders live and what do they eat?   10

Spiders that live in deserts and dry habitats   12

Spiders that live in forests and wet habitats   14

How spiders communicate and explore their world   16

The life cycle of spiders   18

Predators and defenses   22

Weird and wonderful spiders   24

Collecting and identifying spiders   26

Ways to see spiders   28

Spiders quiz   30

Glossary   31

Index   32

Glossary words

When a word is printed in **bold** you can look up its meaning in the Glossary on page 31.

What are spiders?

Spiders belong to a group of animals called **arachnids.** Arachnids are invertebrates. An invertebrate is an animal with no backbone. Instead of having bones, spiders have hard plates and strong, flexible skin around the outside of their bodies to protect their soft insides.

Spiders have:
- eight legs
- many eyes
- a mouth
- jaws with two fangs
- special silk-producing organs called spinnerets
- breathing holes on the sides of their bodies opening into **book lungs** and air tubes inside their bodies.

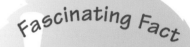

Fascinating Fact

Other arachnids include scorpions, mites and ticks.

This colorful spider is a jumping spider.

4

What makes spiders different from insects?

Spiders are not insects.

- Spiders have eight legs and insects have six legs.
- Spiders have two main body segments and insects have three body segments.
- Spiders make webs and insects do not.
- Spiders have fangs and insects do not.

Primitive and modern spiders

All spiders can be divided into two groups: **primitive** spiders and modern spiders.

- Primitive spiders have fangs that open and close in an up-and-down motion. An example of a primitive spider is a funnel-web spider. Primitive spiders have kept more of the features of spiders that lived long ago than modern spiders.

- Modern spiders have fangs that open and close in a side-to-side motion. An example of a modern spider is an orb-weaving spider.

This mouse spider is a primitive spider. Like all primitive spiders, it has to raise the front of its body in order to bite its prey. Primitive spiders have fangs that open in an up-and-down motion.

This huntsman spider is a modern spider. The fangs of all modern spiders bite toward one another. This is a better way to bite and handle prey, especially if the spider is on a springy web or grabbing prey on the run.

Fascinating Fact

There are about 2,000 kinds of spiders in Australia.

5

Spider bodies

The body of a spider is divided into two segments. These segments are called the **cephalothorax** and the **abdomen**.

Spiders have many hairs on their bodies, including in their mouths. These hairs help spiders to sense their world by touch and taste. The hairs come in many different shapes and sizes. They can be long or short, thick or thin. Some spiders are very hairy and some spiders do not look hairy at all. It all depends on what kind of spider it is.

Abdomen

The abdomen is where:
- food is digested
- females produce eggs
- males produce **sperm**.

abdomen

Did you know?

The word 'cephalothorax' comes from two ancient Greek words. 'Cephalo-' is from the word for 'head', and '-thorax' is from the word for 'chest'.

This is a female wolf spider.

6

This is what the underside of a spider looks like. You can see how all the legs attach to the cephalothorax.

cephalothorax

Cephalothorax

The cephalothorax is the front part of the spider's body. It is a combination of the head and the **thorax**.

On the cephalothorax are the:
- mouth
- jaws with fangs
- eyes
- **palps**
- legs.

Fascinating Fact

Spiders have a thin waist between their cephalothorax and their abdomen. This thin waist allows the spider to move its abdomen around when it is spinning its silk.

The cephalothorax

On the cephalothorax are the spider's mouth, jaws, fangs, eyes, palps and legs.

Mouth

Spiders only eat liquid food. The spider pumps the body juices from its prey into its mouth and down into its stomach.

Jaws with fangs

A spider's fangs are hard, hollow and sharp. Spiders can release **venom** through their fangs and into their prey.

Eyes

Spiders usually have two rows of four eyes.

Palps

The spider's palps look like short front legs. They are used to sense the environment, signal to other spiders and handle prey.

This is a male huntsman spider.

Legs

Spiders have eight legs. Each leg has two or three claws on the end.

Most spiders with three claws on each leg are web builders. They use their third claw to hold onto silk lines in their webs. Some spiders have tufts of hair instead of a third claw. These claw tufts enable spiders to run along smooth surfaces like glass or leaves. Most of these spiders are hunters.

This female huntsman spider sits on a leaf. The claw tufts on the end of each leg help her to hold onto the shiny leaf.

The abdomen

On the abdomen of a spider are the spinnerets and the lungs.

Spinnerets

The spinnerets are where spiders make their silk. Most spiders have four or six spinnerets. On each spinneret are little nozzles called spigots. Each spigot is attached to a silk gland. Silk is made in the silk gland and comes out of the little spigots. There are eight types of silk glands and they produce different types of silk. Silk can be woolly, sticky or in long lines.

Different types of silk can be used for:
- building webs
- making nets to catch prey
- making safety lines
- lining burrows
- wrapping prey
- making egg sacs
- ballooning
- moving around.

A female red-back spider making her silk egg sac. The silk is coming out of the spinnerets at the end of her abdomen. The spider uses her legs to rotate the egg sac as she wraps it in silk.

This female net-casting spider is spinning her web. Net-casting spiders use woolly silk to make their web. Webs made of this type of silk are good at tangling up the bristles, spines and claws of insect prey.

Fascinating Fact

Spiders pull silk out of their spinnerets by using their hind legs or the weight of their bodies.

Lungs

Spiders breathe through small holes in their abdomens, called spiracles. Air passes in through the spiracles and travels to the spider's lungs and tiny air tubes. Spiders have a long heart that pumps their clear, blue blood around their bodies. Sometimes you can see a spider's heart beating through the skin of its abdomen.

Where do spiders live and what do they eat?

Spiders can be found in all sorts of **habitats** including deserts, jungles, gardens, caves, houses, forests, mangroves, ponds and streams. Spiders live in certain places because that is where they find their food.

Most spiders eat insects. Spiders eat by sucking the body juices out of their prey.

How spiders catch their food

Most spiders catch their food in one of three ways. They can:
- hunt it
- ambush it
- trap it using a web.

Wolf spiders are hunting spiders. This female wolf spider has caught a lizard.

Hunting

Spiders that hunt their prey have good eyesight. Some can run very fast and others are very good at jumping. When they see their prey, they either stalk it or rush towards it and grab it. Spiders can also roam around looking for prey. Wolf spiders, huntsman spiders and jumping spiders hunt their prey.

Ambushing

Spiders that ambush their prey mostly sit and wait for their prey to come to them. Some spiders attract their prey by looking or smelling a certain way, like the bird dung spider. Some hide so that their prey cannot see them, like the trapdoor spider. Some spiders, like flower spiders, make themselves hard to see.

This white flower spider has ambushed a moth. When the spider sits very still on a white flower it is very hard to see.

Trapping with webs

Some spiders build webs of silk to trap their prey. The type of web a spider builds depends on what kind of spider it is and what kind of prey it catches. Some spiders, like orb weavers, build large, round webs. Some, like red-backs, build tangle webs. Some, like daddy-long-legs build chaotic webs.

Some spiders build a small net of silk that they hold between their front legs. They catch their prey by wrapping them up in the net. These spiders are called net-casting spiders.

Fascinating Fact

Spiders can be classified by the way they make their webs or catch their prey. The different types of webs built by spiders include orb webs, tangle webs, space webs, knockdown webs and gum-footed webs.

This orb-weaving spider has caught a butterfly in its large, round orb web.

Venom

Spiders use their venom to stop their prey moving while they eat it. Some spiders have quick-acting venom. These spiders often capture prey that could be dangerous, like bees and other spiders. Other web-building spiders, have much weaker venom. Web-building spiders usually carefully wrap their prey in silk before they bite it.

Fascinating Fact

Most spider venom affects their prey's nervous system. This stops prey from being able to move, making it easy for the spider to eat it.

This female funnel-web spider has drops of venom on the ends of her fangs.

When a spider feeds, it vomits stomach fluids onto its prey. The venom and the stomach fluids combined with the grinding action of the spider's fangs turn the prey's tissues into a fluid. The spider then sucks this fluid up. When the spider has finished feeding, the prey's hard parts are often left behind as an empty shell.

Spiders that live in deserts and dry habitats

Some spiders can live in very hot and dry places like deserts. Spiders in desert areas are mostly burrowing spiders. Here are some of the spiders that can live in hot, dry places.

Wolf spiders that live in dry areas usually build a burrow to live in. The spider usually stays in its burrow during the day when it is hot. At night, when it gets cooler, the spider will come out to hunt for food.

Selenops spiders are very fast and skilled hunters. These spiders live under bark and rocks and can often be found on rocky outcrops. The patterns on their bodies make them hard to see. This helps protect them from being caught by predators.

Ant spiders that live in central Australia can usually be found living in burrows. These spiders often make little mounds of soil at their burrow's entrance. At night they sit on top of them. Ant spiders only eat ants.

Did you know?

Spiders that live in dry habitats can dry out easily, so they need to get fluid. Spiders can get fluid from their food or by drinking dew.

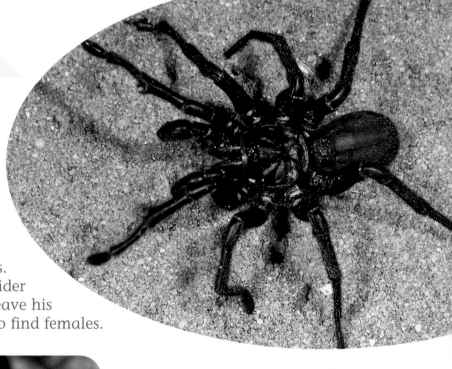

Trapdoor spiders are big spiders that live in big burrows. These spiders hunt insects that live on the ground like beetles and ants. When the male trapdoor spider becomes an adult, he will leave his burrow and go wandering to find females.

Red-back spiders are common in dry areas. These spiders are usually found under rocks or in low bushy plants. Red-back spiders build webs called gum-footed webs. These webs are composed of a tangled, funnel-like upper area connected to lots of sticky lines that extend down to the ground. When the spider's prey walks into the forest of sticky lines, it becomes trapped and the spider drops down and catches it.

Spiders that live in forests and wet habitats

Lots of spiders like to live in forests. Some spiders can even live on water. Here are some of the spiders that live in forests and wet places.

Water spiders live around calm water. They can usually be found under rocks or on logs at the water's edge. They mainly feed on water insects and small fish. Water spiders hunt their prey by sitting at the water's edge with their front legs placed on the surface of the water. If a fish or an insect swims nearby, the spider will grab it. If an insect falls onto the pond, the spider will feel the ripples in the water and will run out on the surface of the water and grab it. Water spiders can also go underwater to escape being caught by predators.

Did you know?

Water spiders have special hairs on their legs that allow them to run across the surface of the water.

Trampoline spiders build a platform of silk with a series of silk lines going up into the plants above it. These lines are called knockdown lines. When an insect flies through the air and hits one of these lines, it is knocked down onto the trampoline web below where the spider is waiting to grab it.

These green jumping spiders live in rainforests. This female jumping spider is eating a young jumping spider. Jumping spiders are active hunters and they have excellent eyesight. Any small invertebrate is fair game, even one of her own kind. Their beautiful green color makes them hard to see among the rainforest plants. This helps prevent predators from catching them and prey from seeing them.

This white flower spider has built a nest by curling up a leaf and holding it together with silk. The spider will sit and wait for its prey to pass by. Flower spiders have good eyesight and almost always catch their prey by the head. These spiders have strong venom and can catch large prey.

A female triangular spider sits and waits for its prey. When its prey comes close enough, the spider will quickly grab it with its legs. The spines on the spider's legs help the spider to keep hold of the struggling prey. This is why the spines on the inside of the spider's legs are bigger than those on the outside.

How spiders communicate and explore their world

A spider can get information about its environment in a number of ways. One of the most important ways it gets information is by using its special **sensory** hairs which are mostly on its legs and **mouthparts**.

The hairs on this tarantula tell the spider about the world around it. These large tarantulas are sometimes called whistling spiders because they can make a humming or whirring noise. The spiders make this noise by rubbing special hairs on the sides of their mouthparts together. These noises may help prevent predators from entering the spider's burrow.

These hairs provide the spider with touch, smell and taste sensations. The spider's sensory hairs also feel **vibrations** in the web, in the air and through the ground. Vibrations are important because they tell the spider if prey, predators or mates are nearby.

Spiders also have special sense organs on their legs. These organs sense the position and movement of the spider's legs. Spiders that build webs use these organs to feel the vibrations of their prey when it is caught in their web. They also help web-building spiders to find their way back to the center of their web and hunting spiders back to their burrows.

Sight is also an important sense for some spiders. Often a spider with large eyes will rely on sight for information. However, most spiders depend on senses other than sight to keep track of the world around them.

Jumping spiders use only their eyes to hunt prey. Once these spiders have seen their prey, they will fix on it with their large front middle eyes. The spider then stalks the prey until it is about two or three centimeters (one inch) away from it. The spider then leaps onto the prey and bites it.

Communication

Spiders can communicate in several ways. They can:
- touch
- send vibrations
- signal to one another.

Female spiders can release special perfumes to attract male spiders.

Did you know?

Adult female spiders have thin palps and adult male spiders have palps shaped like a club.

Male wolf spiders drum the ground with their palps to tell female wolf spiders that they are potential mates.

One of the ways that jumping spiders communicate with one another is by signaling with their legs. This male jumping spider has two of his legs extended straight out from his body. He is signaling to any female spiders that he is there and ready to mate with them.

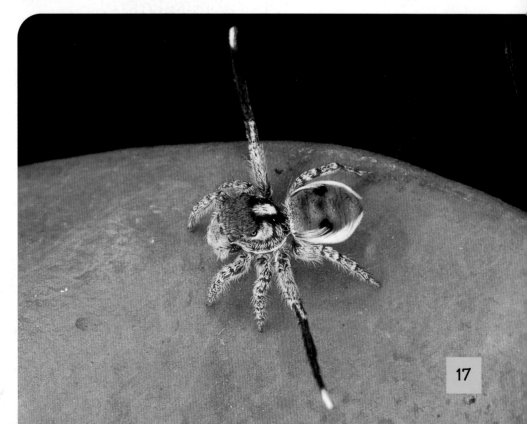

The life cycle of spiders

The whole life cycle of a spider, from egg to adult, can take a few weeks or as long as several years. Most modern spiders, like orb weavers or huntsman spiders, live from eight months to two years. Primitive spiders, like funnel-webs, live much longer. Big, primitive spiders can live for as long as 20 years and can take up to six years to become an adult.

Spiders reproduce **sexually**. This means that a male and a female are needed to make new spiders. The male spider provides sperm while the female spider provides eggs. The eggs and sperm need to join together for a new spider to start growing.

A male jumping spider approaches a female spider before mating.

An adult red-back spider.

Eventually the spiderlings mature into adult spiders. Modern spiders usually stop growing once they become an adult. Primitive spiders continue to grow and molt throughout their life.

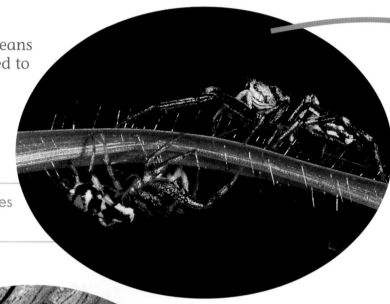

Did you know?

The flexible skin on a spider's abdomen allows it to expand when the spider feeds or when eggs are growing in the female spider.

As spiderlings feed and molt, they grow bigger, like this juvenile male red-back spider.

A female red-back spider with her egg sac.

Female spiders lay eggs. Some spiders only lay a few eggs while others lay many. The eggs are laid in clusters and the female surrounds them with silk. This is called an egg sac. A female spider will usually either guard her egg sac or hide it.

The newly hatched red-back spiderlings.

The eggs hatch into little spiders called spiderlings. Spiderlings break out of their egg sac by **salivating**. Their saliva dissolves a hole in the egg sac. Sometimes the mother spider will help by salivating on the egg sac as well or tearing a hole.

Spiderlings spend their lives eating and growing bigger. As they grow, their skin becomes very tight until it finally splits. This allows the spiderlings to grow even bigger in their new, larger skin. This is called molting and the number of times it happens depends on the kind of spider. Spiderlings undergo their first molt inside their egg sac.

Mating

When a male spider approaches a female spider, he risks being killed and eaten. So when the male spider wants to mate with a female spider, he must try not to be mistaken for prey.

Some male spiders bring female spiders some food. While the females eat, the males mate. Some males have spines on their legs which they use to hold the female's fangs apart while they are mating.

Other male spiders lower themselves down a special strand of silk called a mating thread until they are near a female. When he is near the female, the male spider will start to strum his strand of silk like a guitar. This is to make the female come closer to him. The female will leave her web and join him on his mating thread. He will then stroke her with his long front legs before mating with her. How a male spider approaches a female spider depends on the kind of spider he is. In some spiders, like funnel-web spiders, the males and females are similar in size. In other spiders, males and females are very different sizes. In these cases, the female is almost always bigger than the male.

The smaller male orb-weaving spider has attracted the larger female onto his mating thread.

A small, male golden orb-weaving spider approaches a female in her web. These small males must be careful not to be eaten by the large female.

Spiderlings

Spiders hatch from an egg as spiderlings. Spiderlings look like small adult spiders. Many female spiders leave their egg sacs or young spiderlings to look after themselves. Other female spiders protect and even care for their young. Some females feed their spiderlings with liquid that they vomit up. Some carry the spiderlings around on their backs.

A female wolf spider carries her young spiderlings around on her back. When the female spider catches food, the spiderlings will come forward off her back and feed on the food with their mother.

Fascinating Fact

If a ballooning spiderling is caught in strong wind, it can be carried for thousands of miles.

Some female spiders, like this water spider, guard their egg sacs.

Eventually, the spiderlings are able to go off on their own. Many spiderlings do this by ballooning. Ballooning is when a young spider climbs to a high place and lets out a strand of silk into the breeze. The spider is then carried away on the end of its silk line. Sometimes thousands of these silk lines, called gossamer, can be seen covering plants or fields.

Red-back spiderlings leave their egg sac on gossamer threads.

Predators and defenses

Spiders are eaten by insects, birds, **mammals**, **reptiles**, **amphibians** and other spiders.

Some wasps hunt spiders. The wasp paralyzes the spider with its own special venom and then lays one or more eggs on the spider. The spider will still be paralyzed when the wasp eggs hatch, and the wasp **larvae** will feed on the spider. Spiders are also attacked by insect **parasites**. Spiders can also die from diseases and some types of **fungus**.

The egg sacs of spiders can be attacked by wasps and flies. Eggs are laid in the spider's egg sac and, when the insect larvae hatch, they eat the spider's eggs.

A small mammal, called a dunnart, eating a spider.

A female spider-hunting wasp has caught a huntsman spider. The wasp often bites off the spider's legs to make it easier to carry to its nest. The wasp will lay her egg on the spider and, when the wasp larva hatches, it will eat the spider.

This wolf spider is infested with mites. The mites weaken the spider and it can then be easily attacked by predators or become sick with disease.

How spiders protect themselves

Spiders have developed a number of ways to protect themselves. Some spiders disguise themselves by their color and shape. Most spiders usually prefer to keep away from danger. They do this by being active only at night, and living in sheltered places like burrows, under bark or in webs.

All spiders put down a safety line of silk as they move around. This safety line is a strand of silk that the spider attaches to the ground as it walks along. If the spider is in danger, it can jump off into the air and dangle from its safety line.

If these **defenses** do not work, then the spider may resort to other ways of protecting itself. These can include shedding hairs that can hurt the predator, making warning sounds or biting.

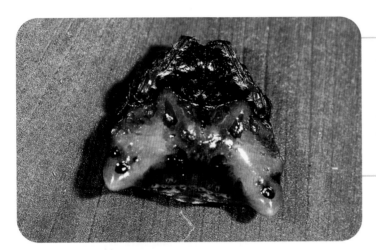

Spiders can protect themselves from predators by pretending to be something that they are not. This spider is pretending to be a bird dropping. The spider can sit exposed on a leaf with its legs pulled in close to its body. It is safe because it looks exactly like a bird dropping.

Spiders can also protect themselves by digging burrows to live in. Some spiders also build a lid for their burrow. When the lid is closed, it is very hard to see where the burrow is. Can you see the burrow in this photo?

Some spiders avoid being eaten by predators by being hard to see. Can you see the spider in this photo?

Weird and wonderful spiders

Welcome to the wonderful world of bizarre and extraordinary spiders!

The biggest spider

The biggest spider in the world is the Goliath spider.
This spider lives in South America. Goliath spiders can grow as big as a dinner plate and weigh as much as 150 grams (5 ounces).

Bolas spiders

Bolas spiders come out at night to hunt male moths. This is the only prey that bolas spiders eat. These spiders catch male moths by dangling a long thread of silk that has a blob of sticky silk (the bolas) on its end. The spider then releases an odor that smells exactly like a female moth. Male moths are attracted to this special smell and fly towards the spider. When the male moth gets close enough, the beating of the moth's wings makes the spider start swinging its long thread. The male moth then gets caught on the sticky blob. The spider reels in the line of silk with the moth stuck at the end and then eats the moth.

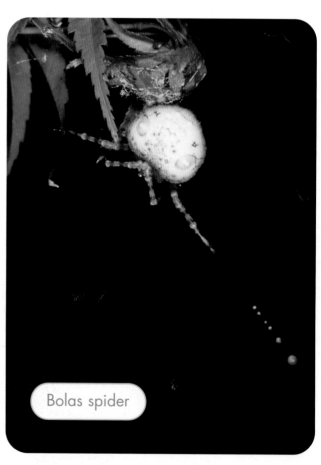

Bolas spider

Floodproof spider houses

One kind of trapdoor spider can live on flood plains. Its home has a main hole that has no lid and a side chamber that is lined with silk and has a water-tight lid. When the plain floods, the spider goes into its side chamber, shuts the lid and waits until the water dries up.

Spiders in disguise

Some spiders catch their prey by looking and smelling exactly like a bird dropping. These spiders put a web on a leaf and then squirt their own droppings onto the web. They then sit in the web. The spider and its web then look and smell like a fresh bird dropping. Flies and other insects that feed on dung are attracted to the smell and, when they come close, the spider catches them.

Scorpion-tailed spiders have a long tail that is used as a disguise. When the spider is sitting in its web, the tail helps make the spider look just like a dead leaf that has fallen into the web. This makes predators less likely to try to eat the spider.

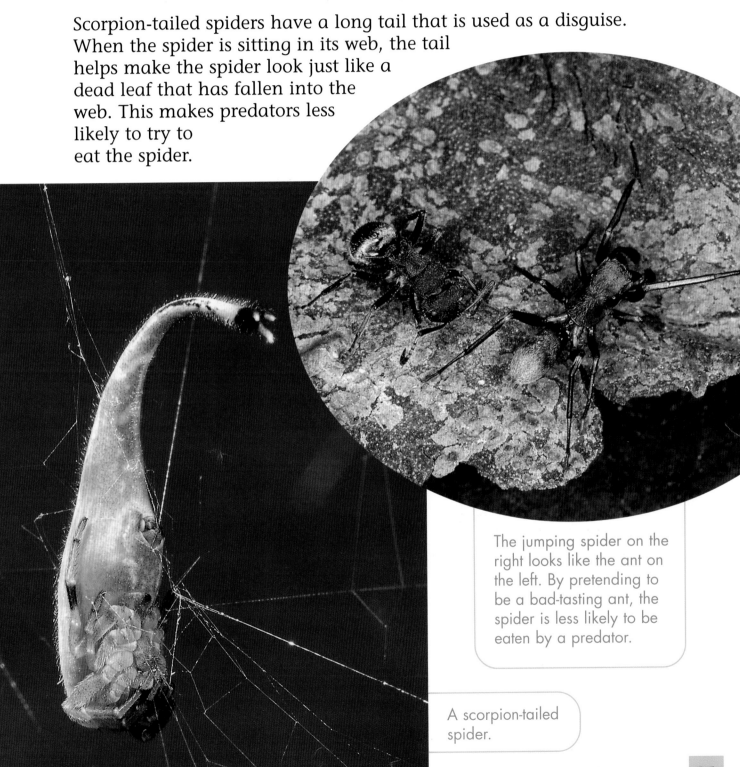

The jumping spider on the right looks like the ant on the left. By pretending to be a bad-tasting ant, the spider is less likely to be eaten by a predator.

A scorpion-tailed spider.

Collecting and identifying spiders

There are so many kinds of spiders that scientists are still discovering new kinds. Some scientists spend years studying the spiders they have collected. If a scientist collects a spider that is unknown, they name it and describe it so other scientists can study it too.

An example of each kind of spider that has been found is kept in collections at museums. These collections are used by scientists who want to study the kinds of spiders that have already been found.

When scientists collect spiders, they use special equipment, like sweep nets, beating trays and pitfall traps. Sometimes they simply catch the spider by hand. As many spiders are active at night, this is the best time to catch and observe them. They can be seen building webs, catching food and mating. Male spiders often go wandering at night while females can be found making their egg sacs.

Scientists often collect spiders by using traps called pitfall traps. They dig a hole in the ground and place a container with some fluid into it. They leave the container for several days before coming back to see what has fallen into the trap.

Spiders are kept in glass jars in a special fluid that stops them from rotting. Each spider collected will have a small label attached to it that has information about where and when the spider was collected and who collected it.

How are spiders identified?

Spiders are identified by looking very carefully at the shape and pattern of many body parts. If a spider's body parts are different to all other spiders that scientists already know, then this spider is considered a new kind of spider, it is described in a scientific publication and given a scientific name.

What do scientists study about spiders?

After a spider has been given a name, scientists can then study:
- where it lives
- what it eats
- its web-building behavior
- its mating behavior
- its relationships with other kinds of spiders
- how it grows
- how often it molts
- what poisons or pollutants kill it
- what its natural predators and parasites are.

Did you know?

Scientists can identify some spiders by looking at their eyes.

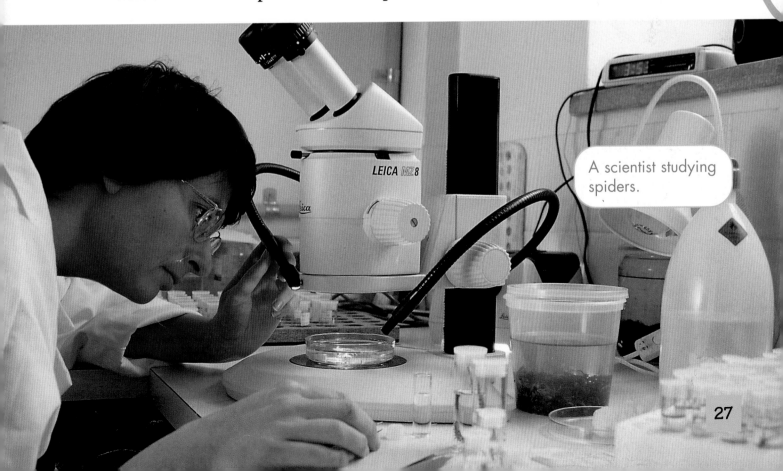

LEICA MZ8

A scientist studying spiders.

Ways to see spiders

We are surrounded by spiders but rarely see or hear them. Here are some ways that you can look more closely at them.

Leave a 40 watt light on at night over quite a few nights in summer so that insects are attracted to it. Place twigs nearby. Spiders will eventually start building webs around the light because they like to eat insects.

One of the spiders that you might see building its web near a light is a black house spider.

Leaf-curling spiders are common garden spiders. See if you can find one around your school or home.

Did you know?

There are more than 34,000 kinds of spiders in the world and only 20 or 30 of these are considered dangerous to humans.

Watching spiders

* You can find spiders, like wolf spiders, at night by spotlighting them with a torch. This is because under torchlight their eyes will glow back at you.

* Look around your school or garden for different kinds of webs. Catch a fly or other insect and put it carefully into a spider web. Watch carefully as the spider rushes out and grabs the insect.

* You will have to watch most spiders build their webs at night because that is when they are most active.

* Watch a spider carefully as it walks or falls. See if you can pick up the spider's safety line.

Huntsman spiders will sometimes walk along walls. Carefully catch one in a large jar and have a closer look at it.

Daddy-long-legs are spiders that you can find in the corners of garden sheds. This female daddy-long-legs spider is carrying her egg sac with her as she moves around.

Spiders quiz

1   How many legs do spiders have?

2   Name two ways in which spiders are different to insects.

3   How many fangs do spiders have?

4   On what part of the spider's body are its palps?

5   Do spiders eat solid or liquid food?

6   What do spiders have on the ends of their legs?

7   How many different types of silk can spiders make?

8   Name the three main ways that spiders can catch their food.

9   How do spiders get information about touch, smell and taste?

10   What are baby spiders called?

11   What is the name of the largest spider in the world?

12   What are a spider's silk-producing organs called?

13   Are spiders animals?

14   What do bolas spiders eat?

15   What is the name of the spider silk that carries spiderlings in the breeze?

Check your answers on page 32.

Saint Andrew's cross spiders are common garden spiders. See if you can spot any in your garden.

Glossary

abdomen	The rear section of the body of an animal.
amphibians	The name of a group of animals that have a backbone and that can live on land or in water (like frogs).
arachnids	The name for spiders and their relatives.
book lungs	The special lungs that only spiders have.
cephalothorax	The front part of a spider's body combining the head and the thorax.
defenses	The ways that animals and plants protect themselves from predators.
fungus	Mushrooms and toadstools are kinds of fungus. Some fungi grow flat on or under the skin of animals. (Fungi = more than one fungus.)
habitat	A place where an animal or a plant lives.
larvae	Caterpillars, grubs and maggots are kinds of larvae. In the life cycle of an insect the larval stage is after the egg stage and before the pupal stage. Larvae hatch out of eggs, grow and then turn into pupae. (Larvae = more than one larva).
mammals	The name of a group of animals that have a backbone and feed milk to their young (like humans, dolphins, wombats and platypuses).
mouthparts	Structures around the mouth that help an animal handle its food.
palps	Small finger-like structures near a spider's or an insect's mouth.
parasite	An animal or plant that lives on or in another animal or plant.
primitive	A kind of animal or structure that existed a long time ago.
reptiles	The name of a group of animals that have a vertebrate skeleton, no feathers and lay eggs (like lizards, snakes, turtles and crocodiles).
sperm	The male reproductive cell.
salivating	To create saliva (spit).
sensory	A word that describes a structure that senses things.
sexual reproduction	When a male and female living thing combine to make more living things.
thorax	The middle section of an animal's body.
venom	Poison.
vibrations	Tiny movements that you can feel and see but cannot hear.

Index

Ambushing spider   10, 15, 16
ant spider   13
arachnids   4

Ballooning   9, 21
body segments   5, 6, 7
bolas spider   24
breathing   4, 9
burrows   12, 13, 23, 24

Catching prey   5
cephalothorax   6, 7, 8
collecting   26, 27, 28

Daddy-long-legs   29
defenses   20, 22, 23

Eggs   19, 21
eyes   4, 16

Fangs   4, 5, 7, 8, 11
flower spider   10, 15
food   10, 20
funnel-web spider   11

Gossamer   21
growth   18, 19

Habitats   10, 12–15
hunting spiders   10, 12
huntsman spider   8, 29

Identifying   26, 27, 28

Jumping spider   4, 15, 17, 18, 25

Kinds   5, 27, 28

Legs   4, 5, 7, 8
life cycle   18, 19

Mating   18, 19, 20
modern spiders   5, 18
molting   19
mouse spider   5
mouth   8

Net-casting spider   9

Orb-weaving spider   5, 11, 20

Palps   7, 8, 17
predators   22
primitive spiders   5, 18

Red-back spider   9, 13, 18, 19
reproduction   18, 19

Scorpion-tailed spider   25
senses   16, 17
silk   4, 5, 7, 9, 16
silk lines   8
sounds   16
spiderlings   18, 19, 21
spigot   9
spinnerets   4, 9
studying   26, 27, 28

Tangle-web spiders   11
tarantula   16
trampoline spider   14
trapdoor spider   13
trapping spiders   10, 11

Venom   8, 11, 22
vibrations   16, 17

Wasps   22
water spiders   14
webs   5, 16, 20
wolf spider   6, 7, 10, 17, 22

Answers to quiz

1 eight 2 they have eight legs and two body segments, they build webs and have fangs 3 two 4 cephalothorax 5 liquid 6 claws 7 eight 8 hunt, ambush, build a web 9 with their sensory hairs 10 spiderlings 11 Goliath spider 12 spinnerets 13 yes 14 male moths 15 gossamer.